Published by Island Books Inc.

All rights reserved. No part of this book
may be reproduced or copied in any form
or by any means without the prior written
permission of the publisher.

ISBN: 978-1-7775652-0-6

Island Books

www.islandbooks.tc

Also available in the series

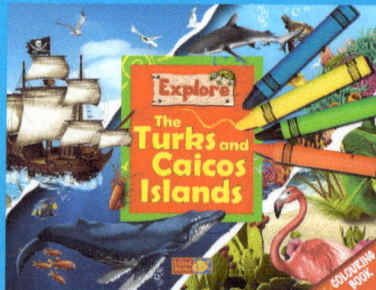

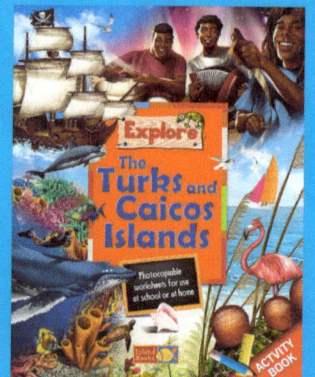

Explore

The Turks and Caicos Islands

Beautiful by Nature

BY

Irene Danics & Katie Hinks

ILLUSTRATOR
Manuel Morgado

GRAPHIC DESIGN
Coral Visions

EDITOR
Annamaria Farbizio

Island Books

Contents

Cross Barren Venus

Lined Bitter-sweet

Sunrise Tellina

Pennsylvania Lucine

Lion's Paw Scallop

Leafy Jewel Box

Common Egg Cockle

Little Knobby Scallop

Zebra Ark or Turkey Wing

Habitats

Land Animals

Oceans

Red Brown Ark

Common Cockle

Amber Pen Fan

White Atlantic Semele

Imperial Venus

Earred Ark

Corals

Scorched Mussel

Coon Oysters

Atlantic Ocean

Caicos Islands

Parrot Cay

Pine Cay

North Caicos

West Caicos

Providenciales

Turks and
Caicos Islands

Caicos Bank

Where in the World?

Imagine living on a small island in the Atlantic Ocean, surrounded by beautiful, crystal clear turquoise water. Imagine a place with 350 days of sunshine and temperatures that only change from warm to hot.

There are few places on earth like this and one of them is a small chain of islands known as the **Turks and Caicos Islands**.

These islands were a hidden treasure until a short time ago. Only since the 1980s has this

tiny country become better known to people around the world. Our islands are known for their *natural beauty* – powdery white sand beaches, turquoise water, incredible coral reefs and amazing weather. It's not surprising that our official slogan is 'Beautiful by Nature'.

You'll see, on this world map, that the Turks and Caicos Islands (TCI) are located in the region of North America. They're in the British West Indies (BWI), which are found in the northern Caribbean region.

North America

South America

Middle Caicos

East Caicos

South Caicos

Ambergris Cay

Turks Islands Passage

Grand Turk

Atlantic Ocean

Salt Cay

Turks Islands

The Turks and Caicos Islands are made up of two groups of islands: The Turks Islands on the east side, and The Caicos Islands on the west side. The Turks Islands Passage separates these two groups of islands. This passage is a water channel – 22 miles long and over 8,000 feet deep. Although TCI is made up of forty islands and cays, only nine are populated: Salt Cay, Grand Turk, Ambergris Cay, South Caicos, Middle Caicos, North Caicos, Parrot Cay, Pine Cay and Providenciales.

Did you know?

The British West Indies is the name for the islands and colonies in the Caribbean that used to be part of the British Empire.

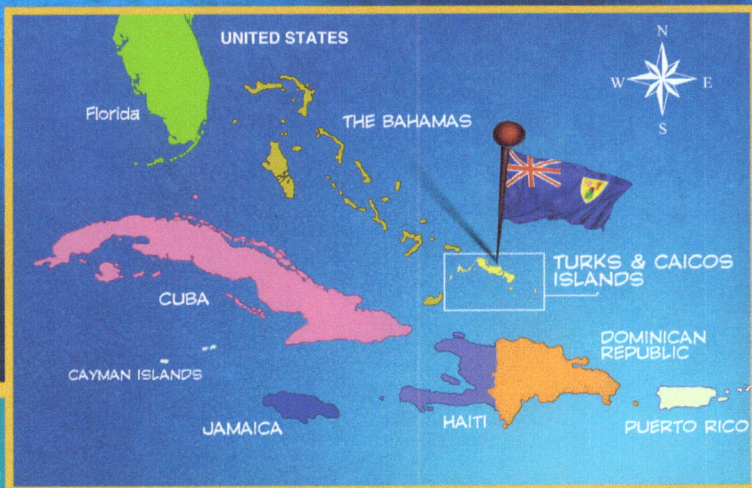

UNITED STATES

Florida

THE BAHAMAS

N
W E
S

CUBA

CAYMAN ISLANDS

TURKS & CAICOS ISLANDS

JAMAICA

HAITI

DOMINICAN REPUBLIC

PUERTO RICO

Key information

CAPITAL: Cockburn Town (located in Grand Turk)
POPULATION: 31,500
LANGUAGE: English
CURRENCY: US dollar
SLOGAN: 'Beautiful by Nature'

The Turks and Caicos Islands are part of the Bahamas archipelago (chain of islands), but are a separate country. They are sand banks on top of huge underwater mountains that jut out from the bottom of the ocean. The islands are encircled and protected by a barrier reef. The wall behind the coral reef drops dramatically from 40 to 8,000 feet, which is almost 1.5 miles. That's the height of about eight Eiffel Towers or 26 Statues of Liberty stacked on top of each other! The reef is like an underwater fortress that protects our islands from the powerful waves of the Atlantic Ocean. This unusual geography creates our beautiful, world-famous beaches and calm, warm water, perfect for diving, swimming and enjoying the beach.

5

Our Islands

Providenciales
Turks and Caicos Islands
British West Indies

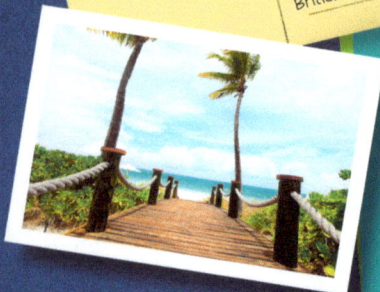

Providenciales (Provo)

Provo is the most developed and populated island in Turks and Caicos. It is the centre for tourism and has many hotels. About 24,000 people live here. Provo is famous for its incredible 12 mile long Grace Bay beach, which has been rated one of the top beaches in the world for its soft, white sand and calm, clear water. The Bight and Blue Hills are two of the oldest settlements, which evolved around sources of fresh water. In Provo, you can find carvings on hilltops from shipwrecked sailors and pirates. There are also ruins of a cotton plantation called Cheshire Hall.

West Caicos
Turks and Caicos Islands
British West Indies

Caicos Passage

North Caicos

CAICOS ISLANDS

Providenciales

Middle Caicos

East Caicos

West Caicos

Grand Turk

Caicos Bank

South Caicos

N · W · E · S

Ambergris Cays

Turks Islands Passage

Salt Cay

TURKS ISLANDS

Seal Cays

West Caicos

West Caicos was uninhabited for a long time, but it is now being developed as a new tourist destination. It is home to many types of birds who flock to beautiful Lake Catherine. Surrounded by gorgeous reefs, this island has some of the most amazing spots for diving and snorkelling in the country. Evidence of native Indians has been found here. There are ruins of a small village called 'Yankee Town'. The town was built around the production of sisal, which is a plant used to make rope. Farming of sisal started around 1890 and lasted less than 20 years.

Grand Turk
Turks and Caicos Islands
British West Indies

Grand Turk

Grand Turk is home to our nation's capital – Cockburn Town - and our government. More than 5,000 people live here. It is believed that Christopher Columbus landed in Grand Turk during his first voyage. American astronaut John Glenn landed here, in his return space capsule, after becoming the first man to orbit planet earth. In the centre of the island, the salinas from the old salt industry can still be seen today. The island is a key location for spotting humpback whales during their annual migration. This island became a popular tourist destination after a new cruise centre was opened in 2006. It is also home to the National Museum - the best place to learn about the history of the TCI.

TCI is made up of 40 islands. Let's take a look at some of these amazing places.

East Caicos

Turks and Caicos Islands

British West Indies

East Caicos

East Caicos has the highest elevation point in the TCI at 156 feet. No one lives on East Caicos anymore but it's home to lots of wildlife. There are several different habitats on the island: swamps, mangroves, caves and beaches. It's also one of the main places for turtles to nest here in the TCI. The main town was Jacksonville, which is now deserted. There are ruins from the large sisal plantation, which ended at the beginning of the 20th century. Here, you can find cave artwork and artefacts that show evidence of early settlers.

South Caicos

Turks and Caicos Islands

British West Indies

South Caicos

South Caicos, with a population of 1,100 people, is known as 'East Harbour' and 'The Big South'. Most of the country's fishing happens here. Lobster, conch and fish are processed in South Caicos before they're exported. Many of the local residents are highly skilled fishermen and free-divers (diving without any special equipment, just by holding your breath).

South Caicos used to be the biggest producer of salt in the island chain. Now flamingos flock to the old salt pans. There are also many wild horses and donkeys roaming freely on its quiet streets.

Middle Caicos

Turks and Caicos Islands

British West Indies

Middle Caicos

Middle Caicos is the largest island in the TCI, but, only around 168 people live here. It's a very green island and has beautiful beaches, dramatic cliffs, swamplands and tidal flats. The island is also home to the Conch Bar Caves, the largest cave system in the TCI and Bahamas archipelago, with over one million bats living there. Numerous important discoveries of artefacts and evidence of life from Native Indian times have been found on Middle Caicos. There are also ruins of an old plantation.

North Caicos

Turks and Caicos Islands

British West Indies

North Caicos
(The Garden Island)

About 1,300 people live in North Caicos and the main town is called Bottle Creek. North Caicos is the greenest island in the TCI as it gets the most rain. Many fruits and vegetables were grown here and shipped to other islands. The island is home to Wade's Green Plantation ruins, which used to be the largest cotton plantation in the country. Traditional crafts, made from straw, are produced in North Caicos. A wide variety of bird life, especially flamingos and osprey, live on North Caicos.

Salt Cay

There are about 100 people living on Salt Cay. It is a small, triangular-shaped island that played a big part in the salt industry. It hasn't changed too much over the years. The centre of the island still has the remnants of the windmills, salinas and a salt house, called the White House.

Today, there are more donkeys than cars on the island and the people are very friendly. It's a popular spot for whale watching and its waters host one of the only diveable shipwrecks in the TCI, the *Endymion*.

Salt Cay

Turks and Caicos Islands

British West Indies

Our Name

The name of our islands comes from the combination of two words: 'Turks' and 'Caicos'.

Turks Head Cactus

Turks

When the Spanish arrived in what is now known as Grand Turk, they saw some very strange cacti. They thought that the tops of the cacti looked like a special type of hat worn in Turkey called a 'fez'. They named this cactus 'Turks Head' because it reminded them of these Turkish hats. That is how a group of islands more than 6,000 miles from Turkey got this unusual name.

Do you see why the Spanish were reminded of the Turkish Fez when they saw this cactus?

Turkish Fez

The islands and cays from above

Caicos

'Caicos' comes from the word 'cay' (pronounced 'key'), which means a sandy island formed on top of a coral reef. The word 'cay' has its origin in the Lucayan word 'cayo hico' which means 'string of islands'. The Lucayans were the first inhabitants of the Turks and Caicos Islands and arrived here about 1,200 years ago.

Our official Coat of Arms

Our National Symbols

TREE: Caribbean Caicos Pine

FLOWER: Heather

PLANT: Turks Head Cactus

BIRD: Brown Pelican

Our Flag

The Turks and Caicos Islands are an overseas territory of the United Kingdom (UK). That is why the Union Jack, the symbol of the United Kingdom, appears on our flag.

The shield has a conch shell, a lobster and a Turks Head Cactus. These symbols represent Turks and Caicos nature.

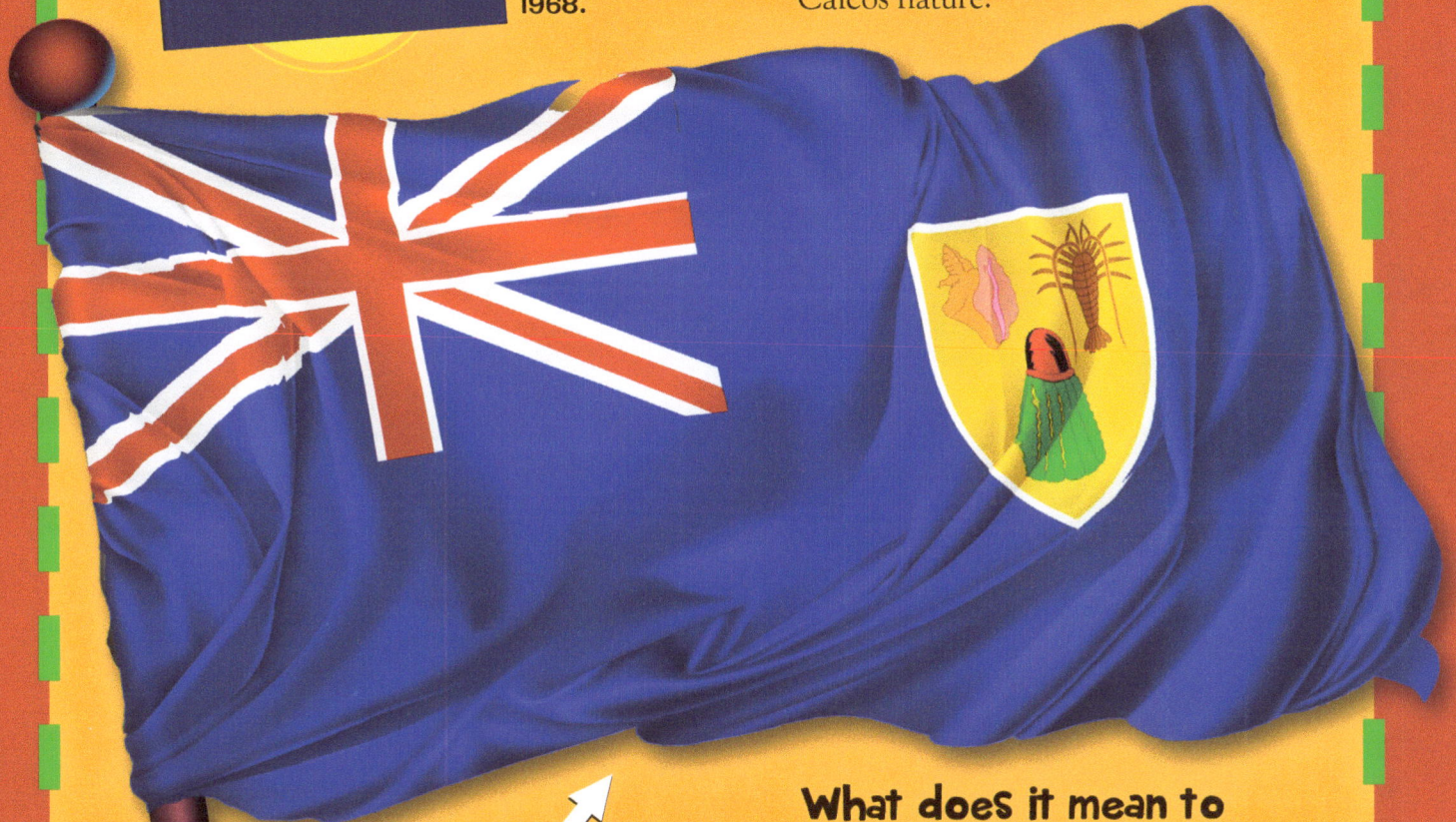

This is how the TCI flag looked from 1889 to 1968.

This design has been the official flag since 1968.

What does it mean to be a British Overseas Territory?

- Our Head of State is the King or Queen of the UK.
- We have a UK representative who is our Governor.
- Benefits: we get military and economic support from the UK.

Fun Fact

The Turks and Caicos flag used to have salt mounds on it representing the salt raking times on the islands. However, a flag maker made a mistake and drew an igloo instead! Look closely at the picture on the right. Can you see the mistake?

TURKS AND CAICOS ISLANDS.

TURKS AND CAICOS ISLANDS.

Did you know?

The Union Jack is used in 19 other countries' flags.

YELLOW
is for the sun shining down 350 days of the year on our beautiful islands and cays.

RED
is for our capital, Grand Turk, for the red Turks Head Cactus plant found there.

WHITE
is for Salt Cay, for the salt which was produced there.

ORANGE
is for South and East Caicos, for the Spiny Lobster and the fishing industry.

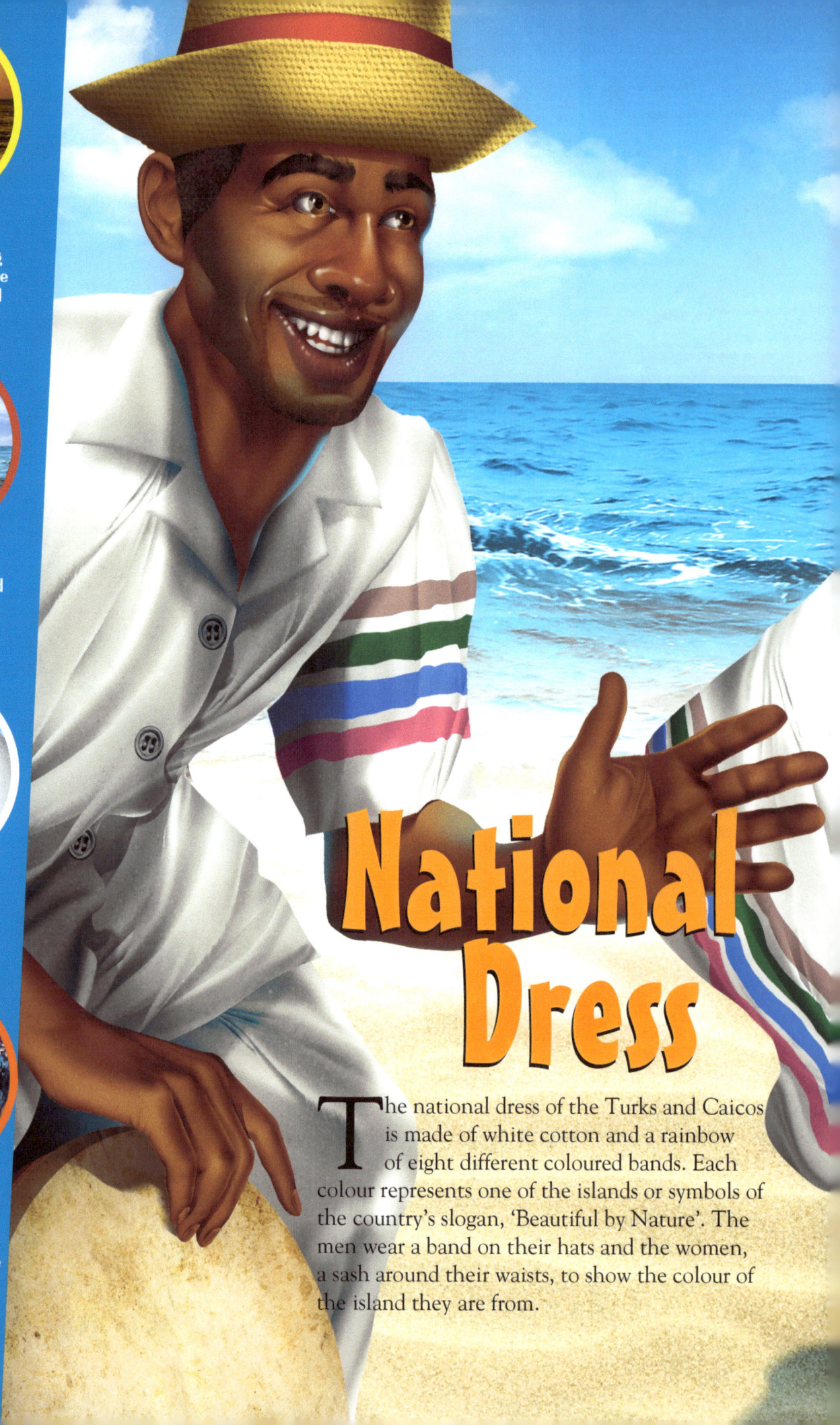

National Dress

The national dress of the Turks and Caicos is made of white cotton and a rainbow of eight different coloured bands. Each colour represents one of the islands or symbols of the country's slogan, 'Beautiful by Nature'. The men wear a band on their hats and the women, a sash around their waists, to show the colour of the island they are from.

TAN
is for Middle Caicos, for the straw used to make roofs of houses, hats, baskets and brooms.

GREEN
is for North Caicos and Parrot Cay, for the plentiful vegetation found on these islands.

TURQUOISE
is for Providenciales, Pine Cay and West Caicos, for the beautiful waters that surround these islands.

PINK
is for the beautiful conch shell, flamingos and the many uninhabited cays.

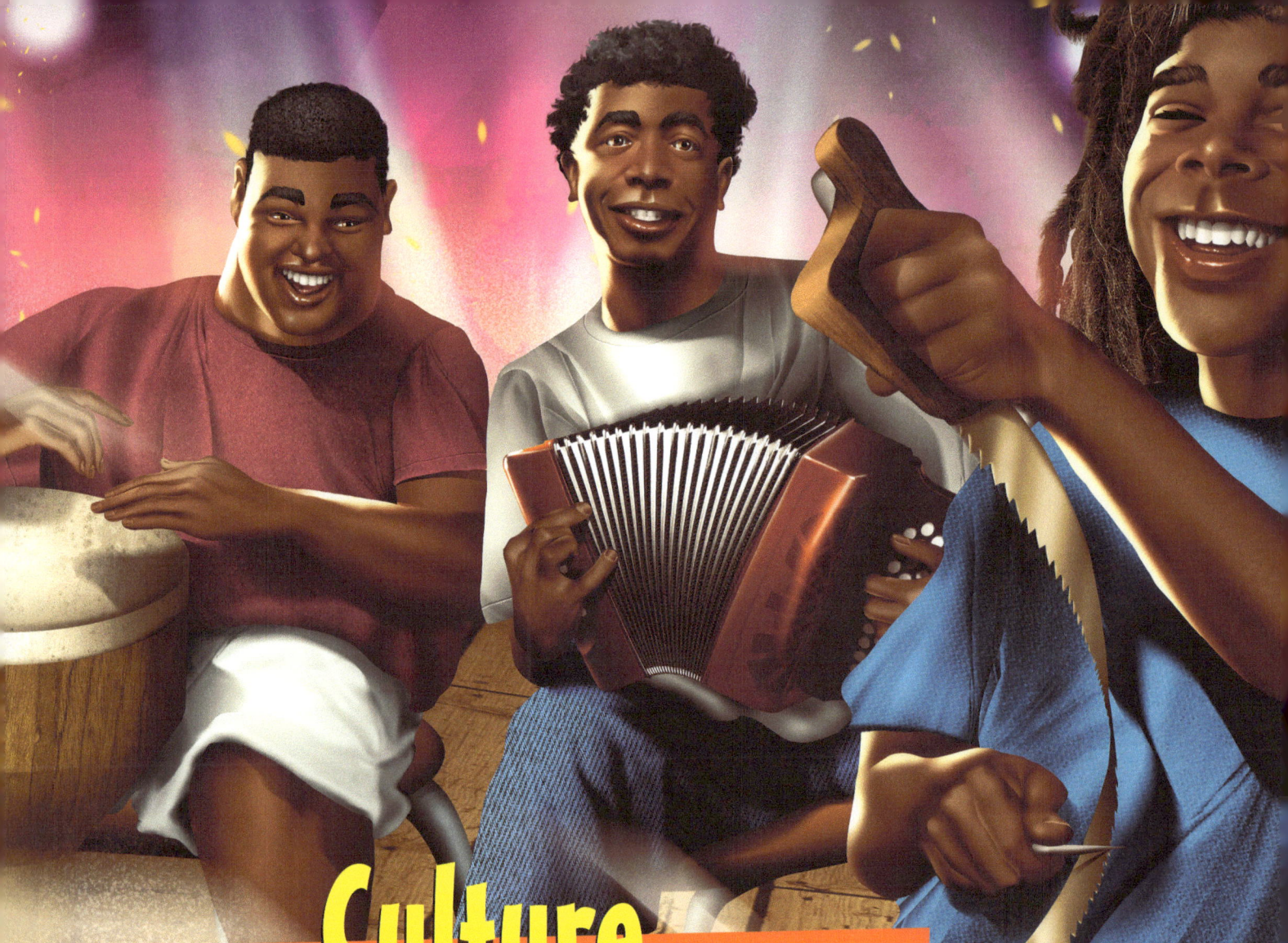

Culture
Music and Dance

Ripsaw or Rake 'n' Scrape

The national music of the Turks and Caicos is called 'Ripsaw Music' or 'Rake 'n' Scrape'. The instruments used are very simple: a saw, a goat skin drum, a hand accordion, handmade maracas and an acoustic guitar.

The main instrument is an ordinary carpenter's handsaw found in any tool store. The musician bends the centre of the saw blade. A metal scraper, usually a long nail, a fork, a knife or a screwdriver, is raked and scraped over the teeth of the saw. Bending the saw and scraping it to the beat of the music produces a distinctive sound, which is unique to ripsaw music. This scraping sound is called 'Ripping the Saw'.

Dominoes

Bones or dominoes is a popular game in the TCI. Four players and usually a crowd of onlookers are often seen around a small table in the shadow of a tree. The final piece is slammed down with a loud bang.

Junkanoo

Junkanoo is a traditional Caribbean musical parade. The exact origin of Junkanoo is not known but it dates back to the days of slavery and some say to a man named John Canoe. At that time, the Christmas and New Year's holidays were the only celebrations when slaves were given time to have fun. They made cardboard costumes, painted them with bright colours and tied strips of paper on top. Participants danced to the rhythm of drums and handmade instruments as they went from house to house singing songs and performing for food and drinks.

Maskanoo

Maskanoo is an exciting event that combines Junkanoo with a Masquerade and musical concerts. It takes place in Grace Bay, Providenciales on Boxing Day. This lively event displays the best of the islands' cultural traditions, including a colourful parade. Participants wear handmade masks and costumes. Loud horns, whistles and drums can be heard long before anyone can see the parade. The excitement of dancing and singing is contagious and everyone moves to the beat.

Check it out!

In Provo, you can sample a variety of local dishes, listen to the beat of ripsaw music and experience a traditional Junkanoo parade at a popular weekly event – the Island Fish Fry.

13

Traditional Food

Boiled fish and grits

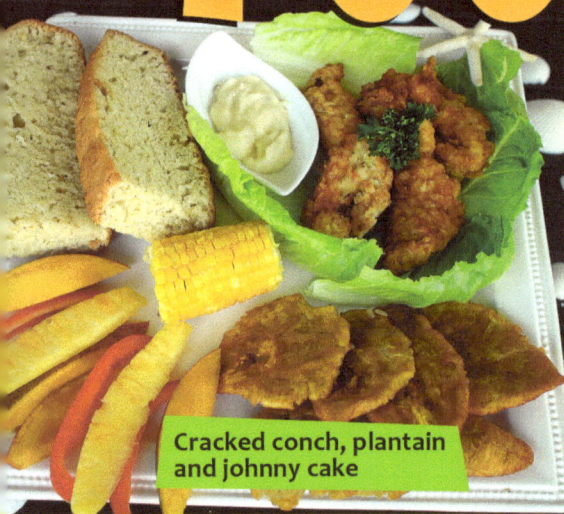
Cracked conch, plantain and johnny cake

Conch fritters

Peas and rice

Okra

Conch salad

Cassava

Lobster

Fried chicken

14

Timeline

Tainos, indigenous people from Hispaniola, start visiting the islands.	750	
	900	Tainos stay permanently and become known as the Lucayans, 'the island people'.
The Lucayans settle in most of the islands and cays.	1300 to 1500	
	1490	Spanish Explorers 'discover' the islands.
The Lucayans perish through slavery and European diseases.	1520	
	1530 to 1720	TCI is mostly uninhabited and is used as a hide-out place by pirates.
The Bermudians establish the Salt Industry.	1660 to 1750	
	1764	The British claim ownership of the islands.
The Loyalists establish the Cotton Industry.	1790	
	1813	A hurricane ends the cotton industry. Loyalists leave and slaves continue to live on the islands.
Slaves become free men (emancipation).	1834	
	1874	TCI becomes part of Jamaica.
'Hurricane of the Century' devastates all the islands from Grand Turk to Florida.	1926	
	1962	The first man to orbit the earth, John Glenn, lands his space capsule in the water near Grand Turk.
TCI vote for independence from Jamaica and remain a British Crown Colony (British Overseas Territory).	1962	
	1966	The development of Providenciales begins, including the arrival of the first car in Provo.
The last shipment of salt from Salt Cay marks the end of a 300-year-old industry.	1970	
	1976	The first self-elected government of TCI is established. J.A.G.S. McCartney becomes the first Chief Minister.
The expansion of the tourism industry in the TCI.	1980s to Present	

The word 'canoe' originated from the Lucayan word 'kenu', meaning dugout. These small but strong boats, made of large hollowed out tree trunks, were used to travel between the islands.

The First People
750 AD - 1520 AD

Who, When, Where and Why?

The Tainos, a peaceful people, were the first humans to settle in the Turks and Caicos Islands in 750 AD. That's over 1,260 years ago! They came in their canoes from Hispaniola, a neighbouring island, now home to Haiti and the Dominican Republic. They were descendants of a tribe of the Arawak people who had originally migrated from South America and then settled all across the Caribbean.

Most of the Taino settlements were in Grand Turk and Middle Caicos where they found shelter in the natural caves.

After 300 years, the Tainos of the Turks and Caicos developed their own culture and language, which was different from other Taino tribes. They called themselves LUCAYANS, which meant the 'Island People'.

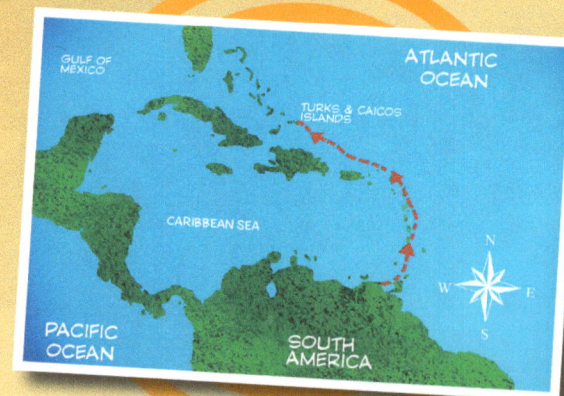

Did you know?

ARAWAKS: The indigenous people of the Caribbean.
TAINOS: A tribe within the Arawak people.
LUCAYANS: The name the Tainos gave themselves once they had settled here.

Arawak canoe paddle

Check it out!

900-year-old paddle found in mangroves at Grand Turk. You can see the actual paddle displayed in the National Museum in Grand Turk.

Why Did the Tainos Come to the Turks and Caicos Islands?

The islands made a good home! The land of Middle Caicos was fertile and good for farming. There were many natural resources on the islands including salt and conch. The Tainos fished and farmed cassava (a root vegetable) and island sea cotton. The long, silky fibres of island sea cotton were perfect for weaving nets and hammocks. Later, the Tainos established trade with neighbouring tribes, including those who still remained in Hispaniola. Around 850 AD, the Tainos settled in Providenciales.

For nearly seven centuries the Lucayans were the only residents of the islands. They lived peacefully and became excellent fishermen and farmers.

Lucayan way of life

- They built circular thatched huts made from wooden posts and palm trees. They slept in hammocks.

- The Lucayans honoured their chiefs, who were known as caciques (ka-see-keys). They believed in supernatural spirits who controlled their lives.

- The women were the core of family life and were highly respected; they could also be chiefs.

- The Lucayans made their tools and hunting weapons from wood and stone. They created a spear from a piece of wood with a sharp tooth from a fish attached to the end. They used these for hunting and fishing, but not for warfare.

- They were peace-loving people and there was no word for 'war' in their language.

17

The Explorers Arrive
1400s - 1500s

The hard-working Lucayans had a quiet and peaceful life in the Turks and Caicos Islands for almost seven centuries. Their world completely changed when the Italian explorer, Christopher Columbus, sailed his three ships under the Spanish flag in search of a new route to Asia. He was convinced he could find a more direct route to bring spices from India to Spain and become wealthy doing so.

After a long and dangerous passage across the Atlantic Ocean, Columbus and his exhausted crew were thrilled to spot land on October 12, 1492. They first came ashore at San Salvadore in the Bahamas.

When Columbus landed in the Caribbean, he thought he'd found the eastern side of India and that's how the people on the islands came to be called *Indians*.

After an initial cautious encounter, the natives welcomed Columbus and his crew with great hospitality. They provided the visitors with food and other supplies.

Sadly, only 30 years after the arrival of the Europeans, the Lucayans were completely wiped out from the Turks and Caicos Islands.

Many of them died from the new diseases brought by the Europeans. Others were kidnapped and sold into slavery. Many were forced to work in the mines of Hispaniola or as pearl divers and died from overwork.

What Happened to the Lucayans?

Christopher Columbus 'discovered' the 'New World', but he didn't find the wealth he was looking for. Instead, his arrival caused the death of the peaceful Lucayans by the 1520s. A unique civilisation was lost.

It was a quiet and sad time for the islands. For the next 150 years, there were no people living here.

Did you know?

Based on Columbus' notes describing the geography of the islands, some historians believe that Columbus made his first landfall on Grand Turk as he passed through the Turks Islands Passage, now also known as the Columbus Passage.

Pirates

of the Turks and Caicos

1500s - 1800s

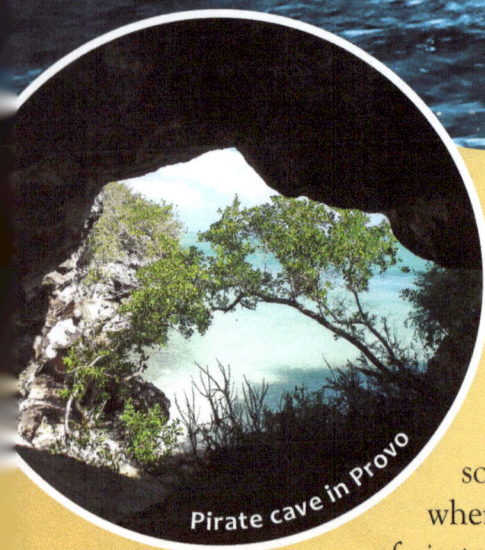

Pirate activity in the Caribbean spans hundreds of years but the most interesting time was in the 18th century. This was a dangerous time in the Turks and Caicos Islands. Pirate ships and Spanish galleons ruled our turquoise waters. The Spanish stole from the Indians and filled their large ships with gold, Caribbean pearls and silver to take to Europe. And where there's treasure, pirates follow! Positioned along the major routes between Europe and the Caribbean islands, the TCI was the perfect place for Caribbean pirates (also called Buccaneers) to set up their base and attack the Spanish ships.

Pirate cave in Provo

Hideouts

Pirates depended on their secrecy, so hideouts played a big role in keeping them out of sight. There are some places in the TCI where you can see evidence of pirates.

In Provo, on the south-western side, there are two high spots that pirates used as lookouts. At Osprey Rock there is a cave with secret carvings, treasure maps and Anne Bonny's name. If you climb to the top of these high points, you get a 360-degree view of the surrounding ocean and land. Pirates may have actually stood there centuries before, watching the seas for passing ships!

Real-Life Pirates of the Caribbean

Calico Jack, Anne Bonny and Mary Read were the most famous pirates to live and raid ships around the Turks and Caicos. In 1718 they captured a Spanish ship carrying treasures and settled on Pirate Cay.

Jack Rackham (a.k.a. Calico Jack)

Jack had a reputation as a ruthless and ferocious pirate throughout the Caribbean. He was handsome and daring and dressed in brightly coloured clothing made of calico cotton. In 1717, he smuggled Anne Bonny onto his ship disguised as a man.

Anne Bonny

Anne ran away from home to be a pirate. She was a skilled sailor and an expert with a pistol and cutlass (sword). She was married to another pirate when she met Calico Jack in the Bahamas, but she left her husband to be with Jack. She had a violent temper and was a brave fighter.

Mary Read

Mary pretended to be a boy when she was little. When she was older she ran away to be a soldier in the French navy. When pirates of Calico Jack's ship captured her, she became friendly with Anne Bonny and Calico Jack and decided to join them. She was an incredibly brutal and tough fighter.

Check it out!

The name Pirate Cay changed over the years and is now Parrot Cay.

Captured!

In 1720 the British Navy captured Calico Jack's ship. The only pirates who put up a fight and defended the ship were Mary and Anne. All the men were asleep below deck and they willingly surrendered. The punishment for being a pirate was nasty. Everyone was arrested and later all the men were hanged. The two women claimed to be pregnant so their lives were spared and they were put in prison.

After a trial in Jamaica, Jack was hanged. Mary Read died in prison. The last thing Anne said to Jack when she saw him in prison was, *"Sorry to see you here, but if you had fought like a man, you need not have been hanged like a dog"*. Anne vanished and was never seen again.

Salt Rakers

1600s - 1700s

Check it out!

Today, on the islands of Grand Turk, South Caicos and Salt Cay you can still see the impressive remains of the past salt industry: many salinas, the Salt House and windmills.

A Salty Business

Salt was difficult to produce:

Sea water collected in salinas. The sun's energy was used to evaporate water.

The remaining seawater was pumped out of the salinas using windmills.

Salt crystals were left at the bottom of the ponds.

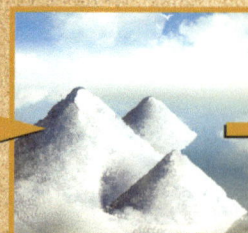

The salt was raked into piles.

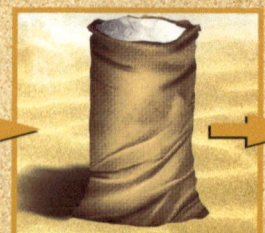

It was then put into bags.

The story of our islands is closely tied to the production and trade of salt. Today salt is basic, cheap and simple, but it doesn't appear in your salt shaker by magic. About 400 years ago, Salt Cay, Grand Turk and South Caicos were among the top producers of salt in the world.

In the middle of the 17th century, the Bermudians selected the Turks and Caicos for their salt operations.

Why TCI?

There was salt water everywhere in the Caribbean Sea and the Atlantic Ocean, so why did the Bermudians pick our islands?

Bermuda is about 750 miles away from Grand Turk and it took only five days of good weather to travel by ship to the TCI.

The flat low-lying areas around the islands naturally collected seawater. First, the Bermudians used the salt that gathered in these low-lying lands. Later, they built low walls to enclose the salt lakes, called *salinas*, and made rectangular ponds.

Slaves, brought to the TCI from Bermuda, were the original 'salt rakers'. Salt rakers were workers in the salt industry, usually slaves, who raked salt in the salinas and got it ready for shipping.

They suffered horrible working and living conditions. The salt rakers spent long days doing hard physical labour in the hot sun. Their houses were simple wooden sheds. They had to sleep on the floor or on hard benches. One of the common health problems they suffered were painful sores on their feet from walking barefoot in the salt flats.

Did you know?

In the 1960s, after 300 years of production, the salt industry in the TCI came to an end. Reduced demand for salt and new innovations in the salt production process in other parts of the world, caused the salt industry here to decline.

The bags were loaded onto donkey carts.

Finally, the bags of salt were taken to the docks to be transported by ships.

Cotton Plantation 1700s - 1800s

Loyalists On The Move

The next arrival of settlers to the Turks and Caicos Islands occurred in the 1780s. With the end of the American War of Independence in 1783, thirteen American Colonies, became completely independent from British rule, and formed the United States. People who supported the British side were called Loyalists. The Loyalists who escaped from the United States were granted land in British colonies in the Caribbean. That's how in the late 1700s, British Loyalists from North Carolina ended up settling on the uninhabited Caicos Islands - North and Middle Caicos.

The Loyalists established cotton plantations on the islands. For several years cotton plantations flourished and produced a large amount of cotton for resale. At one point, Middle Caicos was the most populated island in the Turks and Caicos Islands. Today Middle Caicos has less than 200 residents.

Cotton flower

Blooming

Refined cotton

Finished

Life as a slave on the plantation

Slaves had to:
- construct and maintain the buildings
- clear the land for planting
- plant, harvest and separate the cotton from the seed
- pack and carry cotton to the dock for transportation to the market
- grow food for themselves and their owners
- raise livestock
- worst of all – have no freedom

Slaves

At the time, a key element to a successful plantation system was the use of slaves. The Loyalists brought the slaves they owned along with them. As their plantations grew, they purchased more slaves from the markets of Nassau or Santo Domingo. It's difficult to think of human beings being owned, bought and sold in a market, but that's how slaves were treated in those days. It was a way of life that some people never questioned.

Two brothers, Wade and Thomas Stubbs, owned the largest cotton plantations in the TCI. There were 384 slaves on Wades Green Plantation in North Caicos and over 500 on Cheshire Hall in Provo.

Check it out!

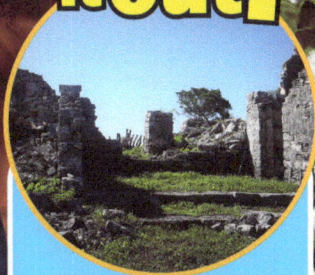

Cheshire Hall Plantation ruins in Provo

The Problem With Cotton

Problems started to surface at the plantations. First, there were beetle-like insects, boll weevils, that munched up the sweet leaves of the cotton plants. Then, the plantation owners found out that cotton depletes the soil of all its nutrients. With each passing year, the crops were getting worse. Finally, a devastating hurricane in 1813 destroyed a large part of the plantations.

All these difficulties were too much to handle for most of the Loyalists who eventually gave up on cotton and moved away, leaving the Stubbs brothers in control of the plantations.

We're Finally Free!

In 1834 the slaves in the British colonies were emancipated or freed. Without the slaves it was impossible to keep up with all the work on the plantation and, shortly after, cotton farming came to an end.

In 1841 the Spanish ship Trouvadore, carrying 192 slaves from Africa to Cuba, was shipwrecked by the shores of East Caicos. The people were rescued by a British Navy ship and after one year's work in the salt industry they were allowed to settle in Middle Caicos. They formed the town of Bambarra. The children of these slaves were the first generation of the native-born Turks and Caicos Islanders. Many of today's local residents can trace their ancestry back to those slaves who worked in the cotton and salt industries of the islands.

Shipwrecks

It's believed there are over 1,000 shipwrecks in the waters of the Turks and Caicos Islands. Many of these remain a mystery.

The Government of the islands protects these shipwrecks and it's prohibited for anyone to disturb the sites. This law helps preserve the objects within the wreckage. The artefacts are extremely fragile after hundreds of years buried under the sea.

Eventually coral starts growing on the sunken wrecks. The new coral community attracts all types of sea life and the shipwrecks become special diving sites.

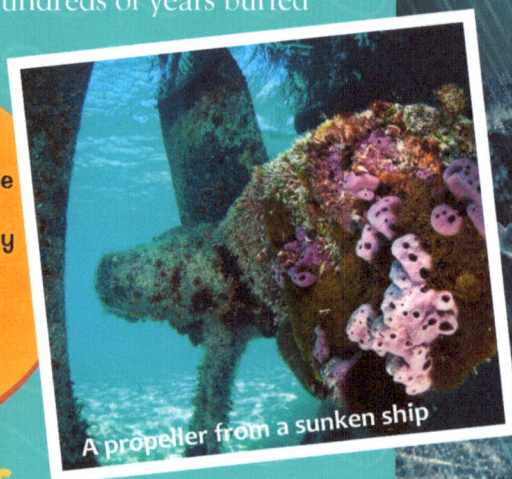
A propeller from a sunken ship

Molasses Reef

One well known shipwreck is the Molasses Reef Shipwreck located near French Cay, in the Caicos Bank, south of Providenciales. It is the oldest excavated European shipwreck in the Americas. The ship sank over 500 years ago! Originally, treasure hunters thought they had found Christopher Columbus' ship, Pinta, rumoured to be loaded with a cargo of 'red pearls'. If found, this cargo would have been worth 100 million dollars! Unfortunately for the treasure hunters, this ship was never proven to be the Pinta. Today it's believed that the ship came from Spain or Portugal. It has taken four years for the archaeologists to excavate and safely bring out artefacts from the wreck. Amongst the artefacts retrieved from the wreck are: cannons, guns, crossbows, tools and pottery.

Where is the Loot?

Very few shipwrecks have actual gold and jewels, but the TCI National Museum sees all wrecks as 'treasure' ships, not because of their financial worth, but because of the secrets they hold. The objects that are retrieved from the wreckage may not seem 'valuable', but the information they provide is priceless. Since many of these ships are centuries old now, the items inside can tell us a lot about people and their lives long ago.

Lighthouse

– A beacon of hope

One of the most notable sites in Grand Turk today is the 60-foot tall lighthouse. It was imported from England in 1852. The lighthouse was brought over piece by piece in the hope that it would save the salt trade. Many ships coming for salt had trouble navigating the treacherous reefs around Grand Turk causing many shipwrecks.

Light Source

Imagine sailors unlucky enough to be caught in a stormy sea! There's nothing more reassuring than the friendly light beam from a nearby lighthouse. But how can light travel so far across the ocean? It's mainly thanks to a powerful lamp with amazing, curved Fresnel lenses (pronounced 'Fre-nel'). This lamp is designed to gather and condense light into a narrow beam.

The Keeper of the light

All lighthouses needed a lighthouse keeper. The keeper would stay up all night. His job was to make sure the lights never went out. He did this by refilling the oil and kerosene in the lamps. The original lamps at the Grand Turk Lighthouse weren't powerful enough on dark, stormy nights, which led to many shipwrecks off the coast. In 1943, brighter kerosene lamps and a more powerful Fresnel lens were added. These changes improved the situation. Finally, in 1972, the lighthouse was converted to electricity and provided a bright beacon to guide all ships safely past the reefs.

Check it out!

If you want to see real life treasures found from the Molasses Reef wreck, they are on display at the National Museum in Grand Turk.

Space Mission

Did you know that the TCI got to witness a spaceship splashdown?

Over 50 years ago, an exciting event in history occurred in the Turks and Caicos Islands.

On February 20, 1962, America and the rest of the world were glued to their television sets and radios to watch and listen to the flight of astronaut, John Glenn. He was the first American to orbit the earth.

From outer space the world could hear Glenn's words, *'This is Friendship 7.....zero G and I feel fine.....oh, the view is tremendous'*.
Zero G=Zero Gravity

PROJECT MERCURY
BALLISTIC CAPSULE

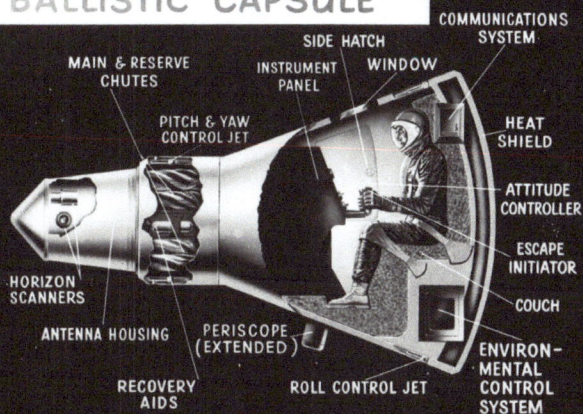

COMMUNICATIONS SYSTEM

MAIN & RESERVE CHUTES

SIDE HATCH

INSTRUMENT PANEL

WINDOW

PITCH & YAW CONTROL JET

HEAT SHIELD

ATTITUDE CONTROLLER

ESCAPE INITIATOR

HORIZON SCANNERS

COUCH

ANTENNA HOUSING

PERISCOPE (EXTENDED)

RECOVERY AIDS

ROLL CONTROL JET

ENVIRON-MENTAL CONTROL SYSTEM

A Mission to the Moon

Lieutenant Colonel John Glenn was launched into space from the Kennedy Space Centre in Florida. He orbited the earth three times in just under 5 hours. His spacecraft reached a speed of 17,500 miles per hour. That's very fast!

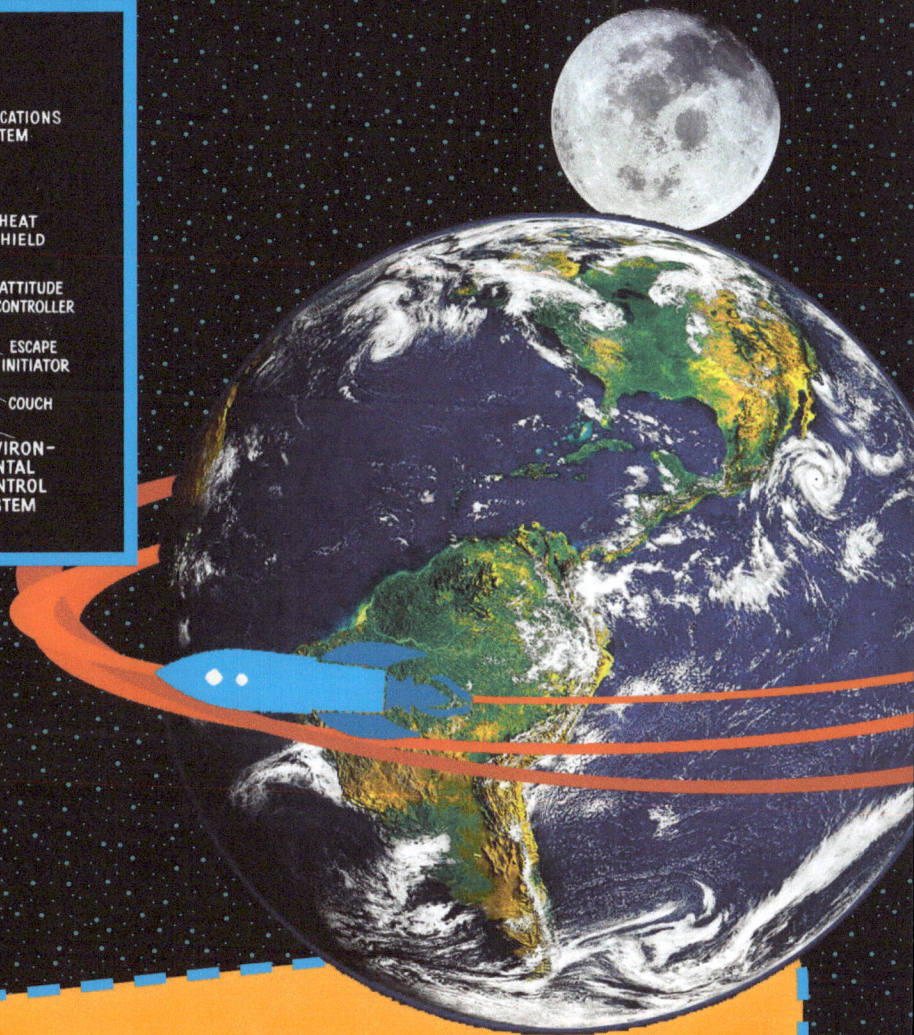

Danger, Danger

Because of a mechanical problem, John Glenn had to make an emergency return to earth. His spaceship, named Friendship 7, splashed into the Atlantic Ocean, close to the Turks and Caicos Islands. He was taken to the hospital in Grand Turk for a medical examination. Lyndon B. Johnson, who was Vice President of the U.S.A. at the time, flew to the islands two days later to take John Glenn back home. This event made international news. Today, if you visit Grand Turk, you can see a replica of Glenn's space capsule displayed next to the airport. Excited Turks Islanders, who had the opportunity to shake Glenn's hand that momentous day, went around to tell everyone they had 'touched space'.

-29-

This is what a hurricane looks like on land.

Hurricanes

In the Turks and Caicos we are extremely fortunate to have lots of sunshine and warm weather all year around. But there's one weather system that people living here are not too happy about – hurricanes!

In the Turks and Caicos, the hurricane season is from June 1 to November 30, but most hurricanes happen during September.

Hurricanes are really big storms with powerful winds and heavy rain. Some hurricanes come and go and really don't cause much more trouble than a bad thunderstorm. Others may damage homes, cause flooding and loss of electricity.

Did you know?

A 'hurricane watch' means that there's a possibility that a hurricane will make landfall within 36 hours. A 'hurricane warning' is issued when a hurricane is definitely on the way and will make landfall within 24 hours and people are advised to prepare.

Hurricanes have names

Each year the World Meteorological Organization uses one of six name lists. Each list alternates between male and female names. If a hurricane causes significant damage, its name is taken off the list.

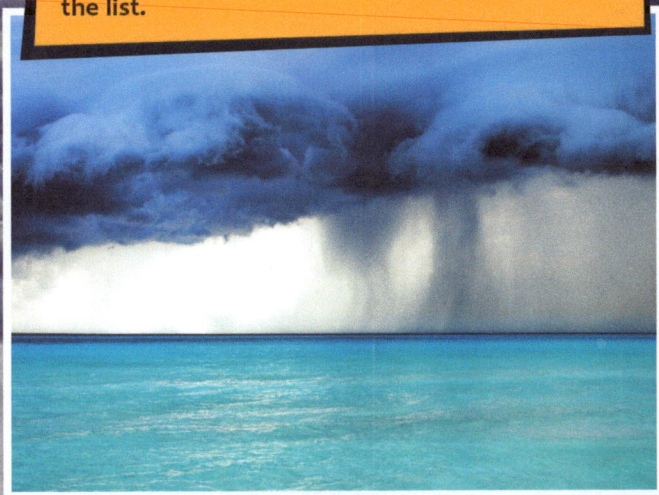

This is what a hurricane looks like from space.

Categories of Hurricanes

There are five categories of hurricanes which are based on wind speeds.

CATEGORY	WIND SPEED	POSSIBLE DAMAGE
1	74 to 95 mph	Broken branches, uprooted trees
2	96 to 110 mph	Doors and windows destroyed, 8 ft waves
3	111 to 130 mph	Major flooding near coast, destroyed homes
4	131 to 155 mph	Some buildings and roofs can be destroyed
5	Over 155 mph	Buildings along the shoreline are washed away

Other names for a hurricane include cyclone and typhoon.

Why do Hurricanes Happen?

Hurricanes form over warm ocean water that has a temperature of at least 80 degrees Fahrenheit. This warm water provides the heat and energy a hurricane needs to grow. Evaporation from the seawater, due to high temperatures, increases their power. Hurricanes can be up to 600 miles across and have powerful winds spiralling at speeds of 75 to 200 miles per hour!

The winds die down when they go over land or move over a cooler area. At the centre of the rotating storm is a small round area of clear skies called the 'eye'. A Northern Hemisphere hurricane rotates in a counter-clockwise direction around its eye. In the Southern Hemisphere, a hurricane rotates in a clockwise direction. Have you ever watched water spiralling down a drain? A hurricane works the same way.

Weather satellites track hurricanes from space. Today, meteorologists provide warnings of where and when a hurricane will reach land. Based on that information, people can evacuate to a safe area when the hurricane is approaching. People prepare for a hurricane by getting extra supplies: water, food and batteries for flashlights. Why? Because hurricanes can knock down trees which knock down power lines. Fixing the power lines can take a long time after a hurricane passes.

They are noisy birds and easily spotted by their long, bright red beaks. Despite their name, oystercatchers hardly eat oysters! Their diet includes crabs, clams, worms and insects. Their beaks are especially strong for cracking shells.

Mangroves

Heron
These wading birds are suspicious and spend much of their time alone, choosing quiet areas to feed. They are very quick when hunting and will stand still at the water's edge until prey comes along. They swallow fish whole, head first.

Nurse Shark

Have you seen tree-like plants growing out of the ocean water? These unique plants are called Mangroves.

Mangroves grow along coastlines, in shallow slow-moving water and only in warm climates. During low tides, their roots are open to air. During high tides, they are covered by salt water.

The tangled roots give mangroves support to handle the daily rise and fall of tides. Mangrove forests reduce erosion from storms, currents and waves. Their underwater root system makes them ideal nurseries for marine life and feeding grounds for birds.

Mangrove trees can survive harsh natural conditions, but the biggest threats to their survival are pollution and coastline development.

Kingfisher
These birds live near flat, calm water so that they can easily spot their prey.

Osprey

Ospreys are fantastic fishers and dive into the water from up to 100 feet using their strong claws to pluck fish from the ocean. They have reversible toes, allowing them to grasp their prey with two toes in front and two behind.

Flamingo

A flamingo's colour depends on its diet. Here, they have coral red feathers. They are highly social birds and they live in colonies that can contain thousands of individuals. Flamingos stir up their food from shallow water and separate it from the mud and water by pumping and straining it through their bill. They are the only birds that feed with their bills upside down!

Turks Head Cactus

Cacti are very tough plants and they can survive some of the harshest conditions on earth. The spines of the cactus are actually its leaves! Because these leaves are so small, the cactus doesn't lose water quickly through evaporation.

Ponds and Salinas

Across the islands of the Turks and Caicos you will find various ponds, salinas and marshes scattered amongst the natural bush. This habitat is made up of low and spiky plants, various cacti and shrub. They provide a refuge for fish and a perfect feeding ground for many wading birds.

33

Hummingbird

These amazing birds are the only birds that can hover mid-air or fly backwards. Sometimes they even fly upside-down. They can be seen hovering around flowers, where they find the sugar they need for energy.

Egret

These graceful wading birds have long, flexible necks that fold back during flight. They hunt by standing still and capture fish with a deadly jab of their long bills.

Glossy Ibis

These migratory wading birds have a long, slim, down-curved bill and magnificent plumage. They look for food in very shallow water and make nests in wetlands with tall, dense vegetation.

Gardens

The Turks and Caicos Islands' tropical climate is perfect for growing numerous varieties of plants. All over the islands you can see colourful blossoming gardens with plants such as bright bougainvilleas, stunning flamboyant trees, fragrant frangipanis and dozens of varieties of palm trees.

Seagull

Seagulls are known to be scavengers and will eat just about anything. They are very clever birds that use inventive ways to get their food. They can drink both fresh and salt water by having a special pair of glands by their eyes, which help them flush out the salt from their system. Seagulls are great parents. The male and female pair for life and they take turns incubating the eggs and feeding and protecting the chicks.

Frigate bird

These birds cannot swim or walk well but, with their giant wingspans they can stay in flight for more than a week.

Pelican

These birds hunt with dramatic plunging dives and use their throat pouches to catch fish. When they drain water from their bills, gulls often try to steal the fish right out of their pouches. Unlike most birds, pelicans incubate their eggs with their webbed feet by standing on the eggs to warm them.

Sandpiper

There are 20 different kinds of sandpipers in TCI. Some are summer visitors and breed here, while others are winter guests, coming all the way from their breeding grounds in the Arctic.

Prickly Pear Cactus

Beach

Where the ocean meets the land there's a sandy beach, low vegetation, rocks and some dunes. There are many beautiful natural plants such as sea grapes, sea oats and the Caicos Pine. There are lots of birds at the water's edge searching for food abundant in the sea.

Four legged Friends

Horses

On the islands of Grand Turk, Salt Cay and South Caicos you can see a very special sight…wild horses and donkeys roaming free!

The early settlers brought these beautiful, intelligent and graceful creatures to the TCI. They are now protected and considered national treasures.

It is common for these animals to wander into people's yards looking for grass. Local people say, *"If you don't want to mow your lawn, just leave the gates open and the horses will keep the grass trim!"*

Donkeys

The Bermudians brought donkeys to Grand Turk in the 16th century when the salt industry was being developed. These animals were used to pull carts loaded with salt from the salinas to the docks. The animals were left behind when the salt trade ended. Years later, when the Loyalists started to arrive, the donkeys were put to use again pulling carts on the plantations. Some of these hard-working animals were busy up until the time when running water was introduced on the islands. They were used to transport water from wells and goods from the docks to people's houses.

Potcakes

Dogs of mixed breed found in the TCI are called Potcakes. Their name comes from the food that local residents traditionally fed to stray dogs. It was hard peas and rice that were caked at the bottom of cooking pots.

It's possible the original Potcakes came to the Turks and Caicos with the Arawak Indians from South America. Later on, terrier breeds were carried aboard ships to keep supplies free from rats. The Loyalists brought Carolina dogs with them. There's also a trace of the African Basenji breed. The current Potcakes are a true mixed breed made up of several types of dogs.

To help stray Potcakes find homes, local organisations connect these dogs to families all over the world who want to adopt them.

Did you know?

If you would like to adopt a puppy, you can contact www.potcakeplace.com. These puppies are vaccinated and sent on airlifts free of charge to loving, adoptive families.

37

Lizards

Iguanas

The Turks and Caicos is home to a unique type of reptile called the Rock Iguana. These harmless, dinosaur-like species used to roam around all of the islands. However, when people started bringing cats and dogs here, iguanas became their prey and now they are on the endangered list.

There are still a few places where these impressive-looking creatures live in peace. Little Water Cay or 'Iguana Island' is one of them. It is a unique island or cay, and home to the few remaining rock iguanas.

If you visit Iguana Island, you will notice the rock iguanas have been tagged with coloured beads. These beads help researchers gather information on the iguanas' life span, their individual growth rates, reproductive rates and their eating habits. The beads are harmless and provide a number unique to each lizard.

Did you know?

The female iguana has a smooth ridge along her back while the male has spike-like scales. The iguana feeds on berries, leaves and fruit and lives in shallow burrows.

Fun Fact!

Reptiles do not produce their own heat. They rely on their environment for warmth. That's why they bask in the sunshine during the day and seek shelter at night.

Geckos and Anoles

The most common lizards seen in the TCI are Geckos and Bark Anoles. You cannot miss these harmless creatures sunning themselves on rocks and darting around the plants.

What is the difference between a Gecko and an Anole?

GECKOS	ANOLES
They are mostly nocturnal and they remain the same colour.	They can change colour from brown to grey or green to adapt to their surroundings.
Have suction cups on their toes. This allows them to climb up and down and even upside down.	They have inflatable pouches on their chins which enlarge when they need to protect themselves or are trying to impress a mate.
They chirp when they're chatting with their friends.	They have little claws on each toe, so they're good climbers.
They can lick their own eyeballs to keep their eyes clean, since they don't have eyelids. Now that's weird, don't you think?	They can drop their tails off if they feel threatened. Their tails then grow back. Isn't that amazing?
There are more than 1,500 species of geckos!	Every island in the Caribbean has a different anole species.

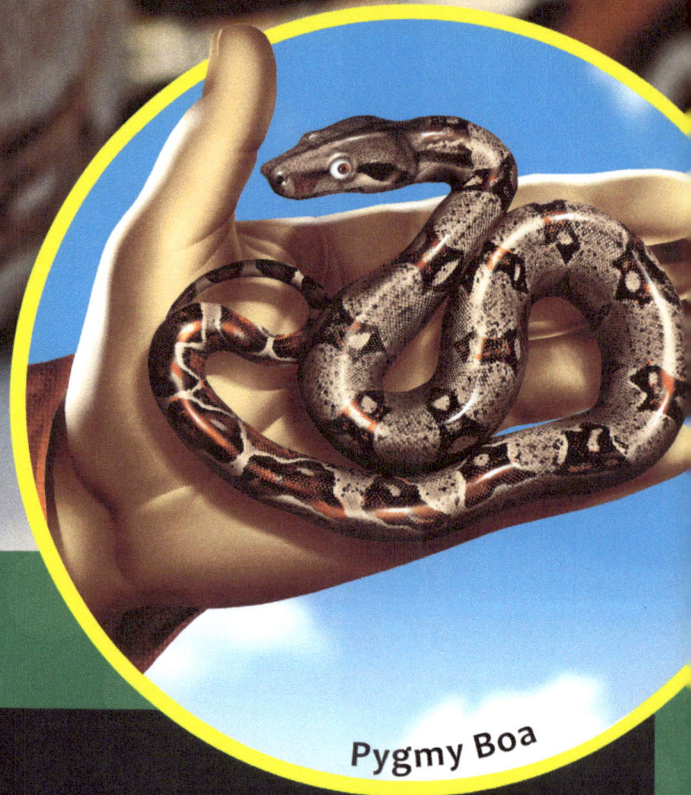

Snakes

Pygmy Boa

We have more reptiles residing on our islands - the snakes. There are three types of snakes in the TCI. The largest snake is the **Bahamas Rainbow Boa** and they are indigenous to the Turks and Caicos. These snakes can't see well but have an amazing sense of smell. Just with a flick of their tongues they can pick up scents from tiny dust particles from their surroundings. They can even smell the scent of mice footprints on the ground!

The **Caicos Islands Pygmy Boa** is locally known as the Chicken Snake. The boa is *endemic* to the Caicos Islands, which means the entire species can be found only here and nowhere else on earth! They are the smallest Boa Constrictor in the world; they are less than a foot long.

Our smallest snake is the **Richard's Worm Snake**. This tiny snake looks like a pink earthworm. It can be found in garden soil. This snake needs to eat quite often and enjoys ant and termite eggs.

Our three types of snakes are unique to these islands and most importantly harmless. They help us by eating pests such as mice, rats, ants and termites. If you happen to see a snake in the TCI, leave it in its natural environment and let it do its job. They are part of our natural cycle of life.

Bats

The only surviving native land mammals in the Caicos Islands are bats. You can spot these fascinating, and sometimes feared, creatures when you visit Middle Caicos Conch Bar Caves. There are literally hundreds of thousands of them! Bats have amazing powers of echolocation, identifying objects by the echo produced by sound waves from their mouth and nose.

In the 19th century, the Turks and Caicos was an exporter of bat guano (which is a fancy word for bat poop)! Bat manure was mined from the Conch Bar caves in Middle Caicos. At the time it was in great demand as a fertiliser.

Check it out!

Middle Caicos Conch Bar Caves

Did you know?

These caves are known to be the largest, most impressive cave system in the entire Caribbean.

Beneath the Sea

What lurks in the depths of the ocean?
Scientists divide the depth of the ocean into 5 zones.

Sunlight Zone – 600 ft

Most of the living things in the ocean live near the surface, in the top 600 feet of water, also know as the Sunlight Zone. This is where most of the visible light exists. The light is responsible for photosynthesis and the growth of algae on which nearly all sea life depends, directly or indirectly. Most of the sea creatures migrate to the sunlight zone in search of food.

The lower two zones are the Abyss, 13,000 to 20,000 feet and the Hadal, which can go down to the depth of 36,000 feet! There's almost no life at these depths and scientists are still discovering the mysterious creatures that lurk so deep down.

Twilight Zone - 600 - 3,000 ft

The Twilight Zone extends from 600 to 3,000 feet down. The light that reaches this region is extremely faint. Here, no plants grow. Residents of this zone include jellyfish, octopuses and squid.

Midnight Zone - 3,000 - 13,000 ft

The Midnight Zone doesn't get any sunlight. 90 percent of the ocean is in this zone. It's pitch black at this depth and the temperature is near freezing! The creatures themselves produce the only visible light in this zone. Most of the animals that live at this depth are black or red.

NOT TO SCALE

Coral Reef

The Turks and Caicos Islands are located by one of the largest coral reef systems in the world. Our coral reef is 65 miles wide and 200 miles long. This reef is very important to our shores because it acts like a big underwater fence that keeps out the powerful, pounding waves of the ocean.

A coral reef is a beautiful living environment. Thousands of sea creatures, big and small, use the coral reef for their home.

What is coral?

Coral is not a rock, and it is not a plant either. It is a living animal that has been around for a long time. Some of the coral reefs on our planet began growing over 50 million years ago!

Coral may look hard and solid but it is actually fragile and easily broken.

So what makes coral look the way they do?

Its skeleton! The hard-looking part that you see is actually the coral's skeleton. A soft body, rather like a jellyfish's body, surrounds it. As the coral skeletons grow, they begin to connect to one another. Soon, they become one living creature, a coral reef.

IN ORDER TO SURVIVE THIS IS WHAT CORAL NEEDS

1 They must have warm water, between 70 and 85 degrees F. Any warmer and they will lose their colour and die.

2 They need sunlight, which means they have to stay in shallow water.

3 The water they are in must be clear to let plenty of sunlight reach them. Pollution in the water can poison the coral and cloud the water, causing them to die.

4 They need salt water, but not just any salt water. Their water must have the perfect amount of salt in order for them to live.

5 Coral needs a base to take 'root' on or there would never be a reef.

Luckily, the Turks and Caicos waters provide these perfect conditions.

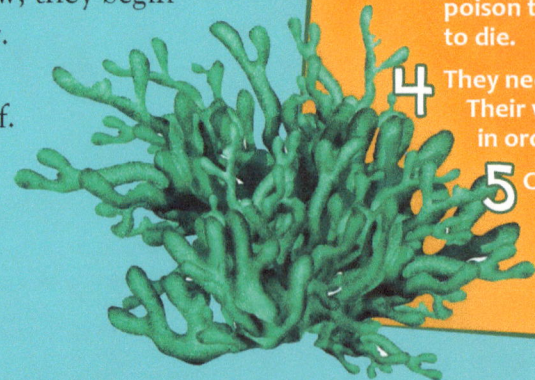

Global warming and pollutants are killing these beautiful organisms. If we do our part protecting the coral reef, it will be around for another 50 million years!

Fun Fact!

What do the words brain, finger, mustard, golf ball, flower, candelabra, sea fan and sea plume have in common? They are all types of coral!

Turks and Caicos Reef Fund was established to preserve and protect the marine environment of the TCI. www.tcreef.org

Working together

Like most animals in nature, coral depends on relationships to help it live. It needs oxygen, but that's kind of hard to come by under the ocean. So it depends on its friend, algae. The algae produce oxygen and coral provides a place for algae to reach sunlight, which it needs. It's a win-win for everyone!

Since coral reefs are so delicate, they depend on us to help them thrive. Fishing, pollution and careless behaviour can hurt or even kill coral. They are also harmed from storms and changes in temperature. While we can't prevent all of mother nature's effects, we can help. Reducing pollution and being careful when diving near coral helps ensure that coral has everything it needs to thrive.

Whales and Dolphins

The waters of the Turks and Caicos are abundant with sea life, but some of the most impressive creatures to spot here are whales and dolphins.

The whale with a hump

Humpback whales can be spotted off the coast of the TCI from January to March. They have travelled a long distance from the icy waters of the Arctic Ocean down the east coast of Canada and the USA. They are on a mission to get back to their birthplace in the Silver Bank, located north of the Dominican Republic, where they will give birth to their young.

Before they reach their final destination, the humpback whales will pass through the very deep Columbus Passage, located between Grand Turk and South Caicos. Up to 5,000 of these beautiful creatures pass through these waters every year. This is their main route, and Salt Cay and Grand Turk are the best places to spot these amazing ocean mammals. While the whales are swimming through the Columbus Passage, you may be lucky enough to witness their grand mating rituals. In order to attract a female, male humpback whales put on impressive acrobatic shows known as 'breaching', when they jump out of the water and splash with their tails and fins. Humpback males are famous for their unique ability to 'sing songs'. They are capable of producing trumpet like sounds that can last 10-20 minutes.

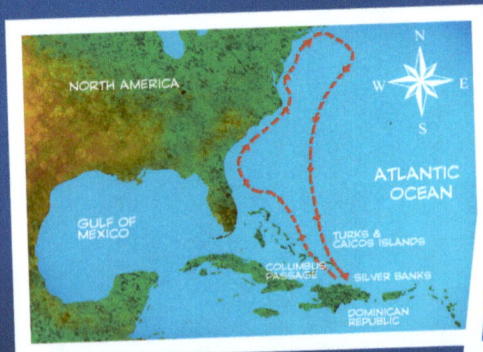

Did you know?

Whales can only have one baby calf at a time and can only give birth every other year.

Whales and dolphins are actually mammals.

JoJo's Tale

Bottlenose Dolphins are the most well-known of all the dolphin species. These 'smiling' creatures of the sea can be found around the Turks and Caicos.

There's an extra special dolphin found in TCI waters named JoJo.

JoJo's story started in 1986 when he met a Californian man, named Dean Bernal. On a visit to Turks and Caicos, Dean was swimming when he came across three small, young dolphins. One of the dolphins started to follow Dean on his daily swims and he named him JoJo. Soon they developed an unusual friendship that still lasts to this day.

Dean became JoJo's protector, wildlife warden and friend. JoJo was declared 'a national treasure' of the Turks and Caicos Islands.

JoJo left his 'pod' (group of dolphins) and loves to interact with people. Because of his playful nature, JoJo has been injured several times by boat propellers and jet skis. These injuries have left him with many scars.

He is one of only eight wild dolphins in the world who prefer human company to that of other dolphins. But remember, should you be fortunate enough to see JoJo, please do not attempt to pet or touch him. After all, he is still a wild animal.

Differences between Fish and Ocean Mammals	
FISH	**WHALES AND DOLPHINS**
Scaly skin	Smooth rubbery skin
Breathe with gills and get oxygen from the water	Go to the surface to breathe in air
Swish their tail fins sideways to swim	Move their tail fins up and down to swim
Lay eggs	Give birth to live young

Sharks

Sharks are one of the biggest types of fish found in the waters around the Turks and Caicos. The most commonly found species are **Caribbean Reef Sharks**, **Nurse Sharks** and **Lemon Sharks**. They are predators, which makes them an important part of the food chain, and the reef would be incomplete without them.

Sharks get a bad rap!

This has a lot to do with the media and movies like *Jaws*. Sharks ARE NOT vicious man-eaters. Sharks eat fish, dolphins, seals, turtles and even seagulls. They are able to defend themselves and have few predators. In reality, human beings are more of a threat to sharks than the other way around. Traditionally sharks have been killed for food and for their skin. Overfishing and shark finning are two of the biggest threats to sharks.

Shark Facts

- They lived in the oceans before dinosaurs.
- A shark's sharp pointy teeth grow in rows. When one tooth falls out, another is there to replace it.
- Sharks give birth to live young called 'pups'.
- Sharks can have between 1 and 100 pups at a time.

Caribbean reef sharks

are known to be scavengers. They are more likely to target fish which have been injured or are in distress (on the end of a fishing line). It is uncommon for this type of shark to prey on healthy fish.

Nurse sharks

like to stay near the ocean floor. They are slow moving and the only time they have been known to react to humans is when they have been disturbed or poked by people who think they are docile. They have little organs for their sense of touch and taste which look a bit like whiskers.

Lemon sharks

are rare to see as adults. Females give birth to their live young in the shallow waters of the Turks and Caicos. You may spot baby lemon sharks swimming around the 'nursery' grounds of the mangroves.

Did you know?

There have been sightings of other types of sharks in the Turks and Caicos, even the majestic king of fish, the Whale Shark, has been seen in our waters.

Rays

Rays are a type of flat fish related to sharks. **Southern Sting Rays** and **Eagle Rays** are most common in the TCI and, if you are fortunate enough, you may see a giant **Manta Ray**. All rays are able to move quickly through the water. These graceful sea creatures have eyes on the tops of their bodies and mouths, noses and gills on their undersides.

Rays, like sharks, do not have any bones. Instead of bones they have cartilage - like you have in your ears and nose. Rays are docile, gentle creatures.

Did you know?

Sharks and Rays have a unique sense called *electroreception*. They are able to detect small electrical currents created from movement of muscles. This helps them find prey hidden in the sand.

They propel themselves through the water with their pectoral fins. Eagle Rays look like they have wings and are flying underwater. Sting Rays tend to spend most of their time on the ocean floor, hiding from predators. As they move, it seems as if they are gliding across the sea bed.

Ray Facts

- Female rays give birth to 2-10 stingray 'pups' every year.
- Southern Sting Rays congregate and can be hand fed at Gibbs Cay, located just to the east of Grand Turk.
- Southern Sting Rays are not aggressive but they do have barbs on their tails to defend themselves from predators. A 'sting' from this tail is incredibly painful.

Turtles

Sea turtles and their eggs were caught and used for food since the Tainos inhabited the islands. Turtles were used for both their meat and their shells. After being hunted for centuries, turtles are now on the ENDANGERED species list, which means they are in danger of dying out.

Sea turtles have been around for 110 million years, since the time of the dinosaurs. They are one of the earth's earliest creatures. There are only seven species of sea turtles and the Turks and Caicos Islands are home to three of them: Hawksbill, Green and Loggerhead.

Hawksbill Turtle

This is one of the smallest turtle species. Its name comes from its hawk-like beak. These turtles are found around the coral reefs. Their beautiful shells are patterned with overlapping 'scutes', which are like bony plates or scales.

Fun Fact!

Sea turtles sometimes look like they are crying. These tears are from special glands that allow them to get rid of extra salt they absorb in the water.

Lifecycle of a turtle

1 Female turtles come ashore at night to lay their eggs. Each turtle will dig a nest 3 feet deep and lay nearly 100 eggs. Then she'll cover up the nest and head back to the safety of the ocean. She'll repeat this process several times during the nesting season.

2 After 8 weeks the eggs hatch. It will take from 3 to 4 years for the hatchlings' shells to change from soft leather to shells that are as hard as armour.

3 The juveniles stay in the sea grass and coral reefs where they can find an abundance of food. Depending on the species, sea turtles will be ready to migrate and find a mate when they are between 10 to 50 years of age.

4 After a long migration of hundreds or even thousands of miles, the turtles will come back to the exact same beach where they were born to give birth.

Green Turtle

Despite being called a GREEN turtle, its colour can be olive, brown or almost black. They are the largest of the sea turtles in the TCI. These turtles can stay under water for as long as 5 hours. Their heart rate slows to conserve oxygen; up to 9 minutes may pass between heartbeats.

Loggerhead Turtle

This turtle got its name from its massive log-shaped head. Along with its big head, the loggerhead turtle also has powerful jaws. Its jaws are strong enough to crush conch, crabs and other hard-shelled creatures.

Run for cover

The 'hatchlings' head straight to the ocean. On the beach they are very helpless and make a tasty meal for bigger land animals or birds. Once in the ocean, the hatchlings move faster but they are still not completely safe. There are many predators in the ocean as well. The baby turtles who survive will grow and mature into adults.

Caribbean Queen Conch

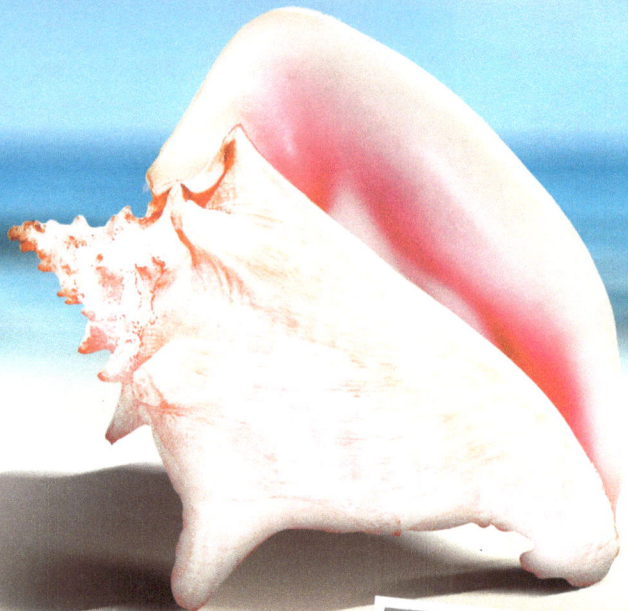

Conch (pronounced 'konk') is an edible sea snail and an important symbol of the Turks and Caicos. As its name suggests, this particular conch is found in and around the warm tropical waters of the Caribbean.

Since the arrival of the Tainos in 750 A.D., conch meat has been one of the main sources of food for the local population. It is an excellent source of nutrition, high in protein and vitamins. Conch meat is traditionally eaten fresh; it has a mild taste and is slightly chewy. It must be pounded or marinated in lime juice to soften it before cooking.

Harvesting

The traditional way of harvesting conch involved picking the conch from the sand bars using a water-glass and a long conch rake called a *conch hook*. Using a small hammer with a pointed head, the conch is 'knocked' to make a hole. A knife is then inserted to cut tendons that hold the animal in its shell. The conch can then be pulled out by its claw to be cleaned and *'bruised'* or tenderised using a conch bruiser.

Traditional conch tools

Conch hook and water-glass

Trade

Turks and Caicos islanders used to trade dry conch with the neighbouring islands. Dry conch was also known as 'Hurricane Ham'. Conch meat was hung to dry during the hurricane months when food and supplies from the mainland could be delayed due to the bad weather. The conch would be dried for several days in the sun. In the height of the dry conch trade, expeditions to Haiti would take 75,000 to 125,000 conch per sloop (small wooden boat), and each sloop made two or three trips a year.

Today

At one time, there was a lot of conch available in the warm waters of the Caribbean. Due to overfishing, these sea creatures became endangered. As a result, several countries around the Caribbean instituted a conch season to help protect and grow the conch population.

Did you know?

The Conch Festival

The Annual Conch Festival is held in November each year in Blue Hills, Providenciales. Local restaurants compete for the best original conch dishes and are judged by international chefs.

Conch Horn

The Arawaks used the conch shell as a musical instrument. By cutting a hole in the tip of the conch and blowing into it with pursed lips, a loud trumpet-like sound is produced. Today, you can hear the conch horn at the 'conch blowing' contests in the TCI and throughout the Caribbean.

Queen Conch is Versatile

The locals and visitors to our islands have used Queen Conch in many different ways. Besides using conch meat in a variety of dishes, the conch shell's beautiful pink colours and natural beauty make it ideal for jewellery and decorations. The conch shells have also been used as construction material, tools and objects in ritual ceremonies.

The Conch Life Cycle

1. The conch starts as an egg in an 'egg mass' which has approximately 500,000 eggs! However, in the wild, only one of these eggs usually matures into an adult conch.

2. After 18 days, the eggs start to go through metamorphosis, which means they change into another form. The eggs are now in the post-larva stage.

3. During the first year, the juveniles start to look like a conch but are only 1/4 to 3/4 inches long. These tiny conchs are small enough to be eaten whole by a variety of predators such as lobster, sting rays, turtles and octopuses.

4. Conch take 3-4 years to grow to about 7 inches and be ready for reproduction.

Fishy Fact File

... except that not all are fish!

Flamingo Tongue

This beautiful looking creature, which is found most often on sea fans, is actually a snail! Unusual markings are not on its shell but on a type of tissue, which covers it. They feed and live on the soft coral.

Spotted Drum

This graceful fish seems to dance as it moves around the coral where it lives. As it grows into an adult, this fish changes and develops spotty sections including its tail.

Lion Fish

Lion Fish are not native to the Caribbean waters and have no natural predators. The spines on their backs are very toxic, so even the sharks aren't eating them! Although they look beautiful, they're a huge threat to sea life in the Turks and Caicos.

Sea Star

They are commonly know as 'Star Fish' but they aren't really fish at all. Most sea stars have 5 pointy arms. If they lose one arm they grow it back!
Sea stars have mouths on their undersides and lots of suckers, which they use to move along the seabed. They need to be in the water to breathe. If you're lucky enough to see one, admire it in the water- don't take it out!

Puffer Fish

There are many different varieties of puffer fish. When threatened, they 'puff' up to almost three times their original size. However they are not filled with air like balloons, but actually take in water. As they expand, their spines stand out like a prickle, which keeps them safe from predators.

Parrot Fish

These fish are interesting as well as very beautiful. Parrot fish eat coral with their beak-like mouths and then poop out sand! That's how some of the sand on the beach is made! Another cool fact about Parrot fish is that they sleep in slimy bubbles. To protect themselves from predators, they spin cocoons around their bodies to hide their scent.

Grouper

Grouper can grow to be bigger than 3 feet in length. They are all born as females and as they grow older many change into males. However, most of them don't survive a long time in the wild so there are more females than males in the grouper world.

Green Moray Eel

These slightly creepy-looking, snake-like creatures have strong jaws and sharp teeth. The green moray can grow up to 6 feet long. Their true colour is blue, but they look greenish because they are covered in a yellow slimy substance – Yuk!

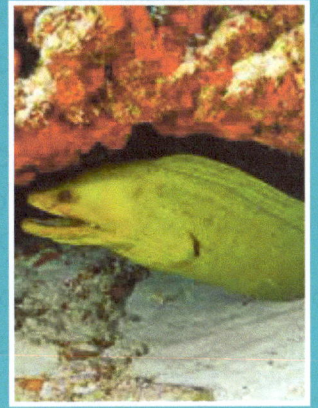

Spiny Lobster (CrawFish)

The spiny lobster is a crustacean, which means that its skeleton is outside its body. The lobster has to moult and grow a new skeleton to fit its new body size. The spiny lobster is fished for its delicious, meaty tail. There are strict laws about the fishing of lobster in the Turks and Caicos. They can only be caught during lobster season to ensure that the lobsters don't die out.

Angel Fish

An interesting fact about angel fish is how they change colour as they get older. Scientists think that the different colours have to do with how important they are within their group or 'school'.

Barracuda

Barracuda can grow up to 6 feet long and swim at speeds up to 40 km per hour. They're known to be powerful carnivores who have very few natural predators. They hover above the reef with their mouths partly open, showing their sharp, pointy teeth!

Sand Dollar

Sand dollars are hard-skinned, coin-shaped animals, from the sea urchin family. They live on the sandy sea floor and partly bury themselves under the sand. They suck up tiny organisms from the ocean floor with their mouths. The white sand dollars found on the beach are just the skeletons. Sand dollars have to stay underwater to survive; they are usually blue, purple or brown.

Hermit Crab

If you see a moving shell, it's probably a hermit crab. This crab can live on land and in the water. Like the lobster, it's a crustacean and carries its home on its back like a snail. But its shell is not attached and doesn't belong to it. The crab changes its home many times as it grows larger.

Blue Tang

Remember Dory from Nemo? She's a Blue Tang. They start off bright yellow but as they grow older their colour changes into deep blue. Tang fish are always on the move and only rest at night. When in danger, they can become semi-transparent to hide from predators. It's like having a special invisibility cloak!

Visit the
Conch Farm

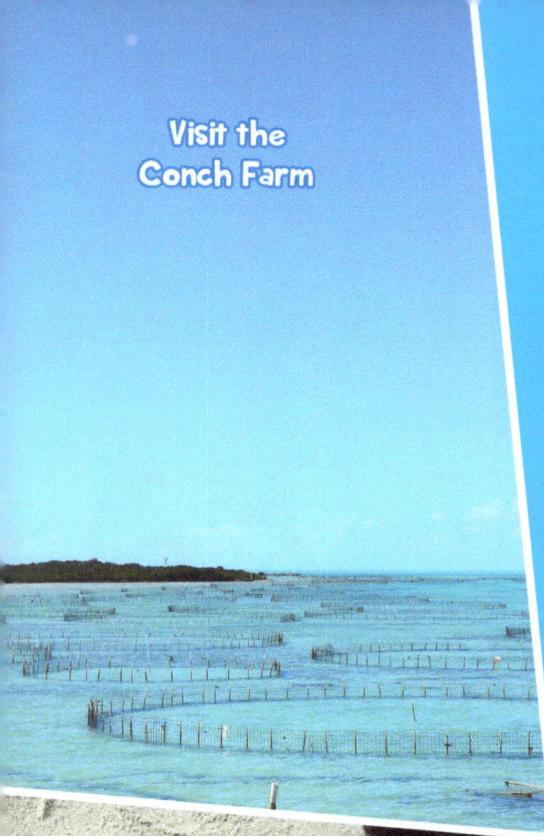

Top 20

Things To Do

Take a Boat Trip

Paddleboard at Sunset

Search for
Beach Treasures

Visit Grand Turk Museum

Ride Horses on the Beach

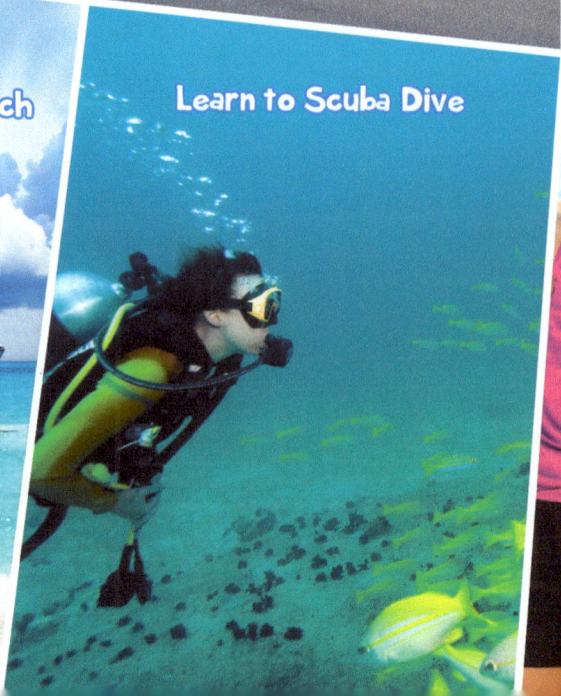

Learn to Scuba Dive

Go Fishing

Tour Cheshire Hall

Go Snorkelling

Learn Kiteboarding

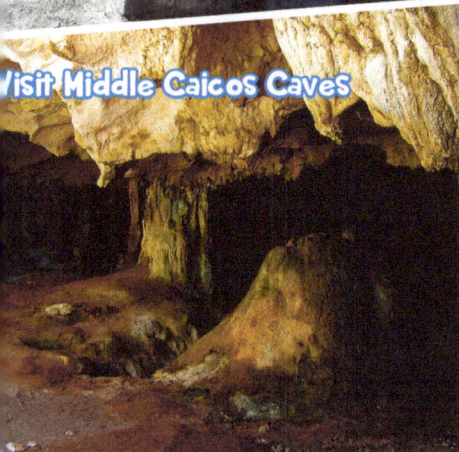

Visit Middle Caicos Caves

Visit Iguana Island

See a Junkanoo Parade

Enjoy Ice Cream with a Pirate

Walk a Potcake

Sail a Hobie Cat

Kayak in the Mangroves

See Whales

Build Sand Castles

57

Glossary

ANOLES – Types of lizards, similar to geckos.
ARAWAK – Native Indians/indigenous people of the Caribbean.
ARCHIPELAGO - Chain of islands.

BARBECUE – Has its origins in the Taino Indian language. Means 'sacred fire pit' and was a grill for cooking meat.
BATS – Only surviving native land mammals in the TCI.
BRITISH WEST INDIES – BWI for short, these islands and colonies in the Caribbean used to be part of the British Empire.
BUCCANEERS – Pirates who attacked Spanish ships in the Caribbean in the 18th century.

CANOE – Originated from the Taino word 'kenu' meaning dugout. These boats were used by the Indians of the Caribbean islands and were made from large tree trunks that were hollowed out.
CASSAVA – A root vegetable traditionally grown by the natives on the islands. Known to be a major source of carbohydrates.
CAY – A small sandy island formed on the top of a coral reef.
COLUMBUS PASSAGE – Also known as the Turks Island Passage, this water channel is over 8,000 feet deep and separates the Caicos from the Turks islands.
CONCH – An edible snail that's an important symbol of the Turks and Caicos Islands.
CORAL REEF – A living environment made up of thousands of coral polyps.

ECOLOCATION - Transmission of sound waves to locate objects. Bats, whales and other sea animals use this sense to move and find their prey.
ELECTRORECEPTION - A unique sense in sharks and rays. It helps them detect electrical currents caused by movement of their prey.
EMANCIPATION – Being set free from someone's control.
ENDEMIC – Species that can only be found in one particular place and nowhere else on earth.

FREE-DIVING – Sport that involves diving without the help of any breathing equipment.

GECKOS – Lizards that have suction cups on their toes.

HAWKSBILL TURTLE – A small turtle species identified by its hawk-like beak.
HIDEOUTS – Caves or other secluded areas where pirates lived.

INDIGENOUS – Native to a specific region. For example, the Indigenous people were the Indians.
INHABITED – Populated, someone lives there.

JOJO – TCI's own bottlenose dolphin, known as the 'National Treasure'.
JOHNNY CAKE – Traditional cornmeal bread which was

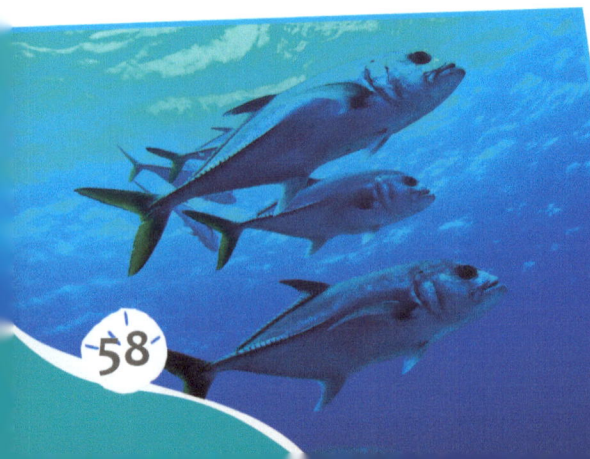

an early American staple food.

JUNKANOO – A popular form of music and parade in the TCI. The rhythmic music consists of goatskin drums, cowbells and other percussion instruments. The musicians wear colourful strips of ribbon and costumes.

LIZARD – A reptile with a long body, four legs, movable eyelids and rough scaly skin.

LOGGERHEAD TURTLE – A sea turtle identified by its massive log-shaped head.

LOYALISTS – People who remained loyal to Britain during the American War of Independence called the Revolutionary War.

LUCAYANS – The name the Tainos gave themselves once they settled in the Turks and Caicos and the Bahamas.

MASKANOO – Street parade taking place on Boxing Day where participants dress in colourful costumes, play traditional music and dance. It's a combination of a masquerade, junkanoo and musical concerts.

MIDDLE CAICOS CONCH BAR CAVES – The largest, most impressive cave system in the entire Caribbean.

MIGRATION – The seasonal movement of animals over long distances.

MOLASSES REEF SHIPWRECK – Oldest scientifically excavated European shipwreck in the Americas.

POTCAKES – Local dogs who are a mixed breed. Their name comes from the hard peas and rice that were caked at the bottom of cooking pots. This was the food that locals gave to stray dogs.

RAYS – A type of flat fish related to sharks.

REPTILES – Cold blooded animals, such as snakes, lizards, turtles and crocodiles. They have dry scaly skin and lay eggs on land.

RIPPING THE SAW – Making musical sounds using a metal scraper over a saw's teeth. Can be done using a nail, screwdriver or knife.

RIPSAW – National music of the Turks and Caicos, also known as 'Rake 'n' Scrape'. The instruments used to make ripsaw music are: the saw, the goatskin drum, the accordion, the maracas and the acoustic guitar.

SALINAS – Low-lying natural or man-made area used to collect salt water for salt making.

SALT RAKERS – Workers in the Salt industry, usually slaves, who raked salt and got it ready for shipping on Grand Turk, Salt Cay and South Caicos.

SHARK FINNING – The practice of slicing off the shark's fins while the shark is still alive and throwing the rest of its body back into the ocean. It's estimated that around 100 million sharks are killed every year for their fins.

SISAL – A plant grown for export. Its fibres were used for making rope.

SLOOP – A small wooden sail boat with a single mast.

TAINOS – A tribe of people who lived in the TCI. They were descended from the Arawak tribe.

UNION JACK – A symbol on a flag that represents the United Kingdom.

Credits

Davies, Julia and Phil. The Turks and Caicos Islands, Beautiful by Nature, Macmillan Education, 2000.
Sandler, N. A Guide to the Turks and Caicos National Museum, Turks and Caicos National Museum, 2001.
Sandler, N. Slave History in the Turks and Caicos Islands. Turks and Caicos National Museum, 2004.

Websites
Carlson, Betsy. "Boat Trips". The Times of the Islands, Fall 2006.
Hitch, Neal. "Vanishing Culture". Times of the Islands. Winter 2008/2009.
Morvan, Chris. "There's Gold in Them There Mounds". Times of the Islands, Spring 2013.
Naqqi Manco, Bryan. "Our Boa Belongers." Times of the Islands. Fall 2006.
Turks and Caicos Magazine. "Astronaut Anniversary". Turks and Caicos Magazine, Spring 2012.
Williams, Sherlin. "Danielle's Dream". Times of the Islands. Fall 2012.
Woodford, Chris. "Fresnel Lenses." Explain that Stuff! November 2013. <www.explainthatstuff.com/fresnel-lenses.html>

The following reference sources were particularly helpful.
The Dean and JoJo Story. 2007. <www.deanandjojostory.com>
Turks and Caicos National Museum. <www.tcmuseum.org>
Visit Turks and Caicos Islands. <www.visittci.com>
Turks and Caicos Islands. Official Tourism Website. <www.turksandcaicostourism.com/songs-of-the-island.html>
The Conch Farm Visitor Centre Exhibit
The TCI 2012 census results
National Geographic <www.nationalgeographic.com>

Special Thanks to the former Director of Culture, David Bowen for his wealth of information on the history and culture of the islands. For his encouragement and support with this project and assisting us with photos and information gaps.

The authors wish to express their sincere thanks to the people who have helped us along the way putting this book together and bringing our vision to reality. The people who helped us with designing, proofreading, content ideas and page layouts: Emir Mesic, Judy Clark, Sandy Lee, Sophie Baker, Gemma Handy and Mary Bergin.

Finally, we would like to thank our families, whose support and encouragement made it all possible!

Photo credits
Shutterstock:
3. Earth 3D: Anton Balazh; 4. Provo :BlueOrange Studio; Reef: Leonardo Gonzalez; Grand Turk: Ramunas Bruzas; 5. Sisal: Nancy Antico; Fish: Angel DiBilio; Flamingo Vadim Petrakov; Donkey: DragoNika; Stamps: brandonht Jim Pruitt, Olga Popova, rook76catwalkerEtiAmmos; 6. Turks Head Cactus: Steve Heap; Pelican: Phillip W. Kirkland; 8. Conch salad: Chiyacat; 12. Salina: Allen Furmanski; 13. Cotton: sursad, Portia de Castro, optimarc; 14. Propeller: Ethan Daniels; 16. Hurricane: Guido Amrein; Storm from space: Denis Tabler; Storm approaching Florida: Harvepino; Palm tree: B747; 17. Kingfisher: Feng Yu; 18. Frigate bird: Nancy Antico; Glossy Ibis: LeonP; 19. Horses: Ramunas Bruzas; 20. Gecko: lupugabriela; Iguana: Christopher Baker; 21. Snake: Gary Boisvert; Bats: Ethan Daniels; Conch Bar Caves: Karen Wunderman; 24. Whale's tail: Cedric Weber; 25. Reef Shark: Matt9122; Lemon Shark: frantisekhojdysz; Nurse shark : Shane Gross; 26. Hawksbill turtle: Rich Carey; Loggerhead: Khoroshunova Olga; Green turtle: Peter Leahy; 27. Conch: Amanda Nicholls; Conch jewelry – FineShine; 28. Parrot Fish – Tharapong Talubnak; Sea Star: Pakhnyushcha; star-fish-Márcio Cabral de Moura; Hermit Crab: alexsvirid; Lion Fish: aastock; Puffer fish: Beth Swanson; Spotted drum: Amanda Nicholls; Barracuda: kaschibo; Grouper: Matt9122; Eel: Brian Lasenby; Flamingo tongue: James Fatherree; 29. Egret: Ammit Jack; Osprey: Anatoliy Lukich; Ship: eAlisa; Gecko: Rose Thompson; Sea fan: think4photop; Bruno Laveissiere; Turtle: Rich Carey; Dolphin: Ethan Daniels; Palm tree: aragami12345s; 30.Ray: Rich Carey; 7. Dominoes: Tibi Popescu/iStockphotos; 8. Local Dishes: Kandi Hariraj; Cassava: hemeroskopion /iStockphoto; Okra: bhofack2 /iStockphoto; 15. The Mercury Capsule, America's first true spacecraft, shown in a cutaway drawing made in January 1960. (NASA photo no. M-278, ASTRO 17). NASA image: recovery of Freedom 7; 18. Sandpiper: By Mike's Birds (Least Sandpiper by Magnus Manske/Creative Commons; 19. Potcakes : Lynn Robinson and Michelle Ross; NASA image courtesy Jeff Schmaltz; 56. Horseriding: Ramunas Bruzas; 4-5. 3D map: Blender Freelance

www.ingramcontent.com/pod-product-compliance
Lightning Source LLC
Chambersburg PA
CBHW061354090426
42739CB00002B/20